How To Select Kurti That Sells Fast

5 Golden Rules for Minimizing Dead Stock

How To **Select Kurti** That Sells Fast

5 Golden Rules for Minimizing Dead Stock

Naveen N Banura

The Women's Fashion Expert

Worldwide Published by

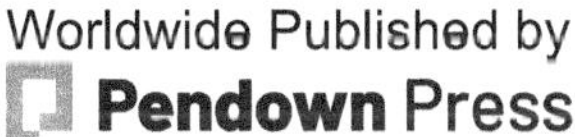 **Pendown** Press

PENDOWN PRESS LLP
An ISO 9001 & ISO 14001 Certified Co.,
Regd. Office: 2525/193, 1st Floor, Onkar Nagar-A,
Tri Nagar, Delhi-110035
Ph.: 09350849407, 09312235086
E-mail: info@pendownpress.com
Branch Office: 1A/2A, 20, Hari Sadan, Ansari Road,
Daryaganj, New Delhi-110002
Ph.: 011-45794768
Website: PendownPress.com

First Edition: 2024
Price: ₹699/-
ISBN: 978-93-5554-891-7

Layout and Cover Designed by Pendown Graphics Team
Printed and Bound in India by Thomson Press India Ltd.

Contents

Preface

In the busy streets of textile markets and the constantly changing world of fashion retail, the kurti has proven itself as a must-have clothing item for women from all walks of life. It's a versatile garment that mixes traditional and modern styles, giving retailers a great chance to build a successful business. To do that, they need to know how to pick the right ones, market them well, and understand what customers like. It is this gap in knowledge and practice that inspired the creation of this guide: "How to Select Kurti, That Sells Fast."

This book is born out of a series of conversations with successful retailers, manufacturers, designers, and customers, woven together with years of observation and industry-specific research. It's full of helpful tips and advice made just for store owners who want to stand out in the competitive world of fashion retailing.

The aim of this guide is clear and important: to help you, the retailer, with the acumen to select kurtis that not only sell fast but also build the foundation of a loyal customer base and a brand that resonates with quality and style. We delve into the heart of what makes a kurti desirable, exploring the fabric, the cut, the design, and, importantly, what's popular in the market.

We'll look at the importance of understanding your customer, their needs, and how to match your products with the pulse of the market. You'll learn how to pick both timeless favorites and trendy items, creating a collection that appeals to all kinds of shoppers, whether they come to your store or visit your website.

And there's more to this guide than just selection. We'll also talk about sourcing, pricing, marketing, and sales strategies. We've used real stories and examples to help you avoid common mistakes and turn challenges into opportunities for success.

Whether you are new to the world of fashion retail or are looking to up your game, this guide is designed to be your companion in the journey towards a successful kurti retail business. It's an invitation to transform your approach, refine your selection, and revolutionise your sales.

Welcome to the path of informed retailing. Welcome to success!

Naveen N Banura
The Women's Fashion Expert

About This Book

This book is your key to unlocking the secrets of selecting, showcasing, and selling kurtis that customers love and buy quickly. It's packed with tips on understanding customer desires, quality selection, and the latest trends, ensuring you stay ahead in the competitive fashion market. By turning these insights into action, you'll not only boost your sales but also build a beloved brand. Start your journey to becoming a top kurti retailer with this essential guide.

This book doesn't just stop at how to select kurtis; it extends into how to become a brand that resonates with quality and style, ensuring your place in the competitive market of fashion retail. Your journey to retail excellence begins here. With this book as your guide, you're not just selecting kurtis; you're curating experiences, building relationships, and setting the stage for unparalleled success.

About Me

Hi there! I'm Naveen Nagarmal Banura, and I proudly call the vibrant Pink City of Jaipur in Rajasthan, India, my home. With over two decades in the fashion industry, I've been helping retailers thrive in their businesses. I lead M.N. Fashions, known as the top B2B brand for women's ethnic wear in India. Along my journey, I've earned a reputation as a savvy strategist in women's ethnic fashion and have been honoured with the title "Icon of Ethnic Garment Industry."

In my 21 years in the industry, I've assisted over a thousand store owners in boosting their profits with the strategies shared in my two books. Despite a successful start, I faced setbacks. But instead of giving up, I took those lessons, stayed resilient, and after much study, research, and investment, I developed a successful framework for retailers.

You might be curious: Why have I decided to write a book? The reason is heartfelt—I want to give back to the community that has given me so much. I'm filled with gratitude for my team, retailers, suppliers, and peers, who have consistently supported me and helped me establish my name in the Indian ethnic wear scene.

This book is my promise to you—that your business can undergo a remarkable transformation and potentially grow tenfold. It's about making business fun, fulfilling, and a step closer to the life you've always wanted, simply by applying the lessons within these pages.

My mission? To elevate the Indian women's apparel sector to peak profitability and scalability. And in doing so, I aim to uplift 1 lakh retailers along the way.

I've decided to gather all my knowledge and experiences into this book, to extend the ladder of success to you. If you're in this industry and not keeping up with the latest trends, you're on a tricky path. Many apparel businesses struggle because they fail to adapt, leading to difficulties in passing on legacies to the next generation.

So, I invite you now to seize the opportunity before you. This book isn't just for reading—it's for taking action towards becoming a top retailer. Imagine the growth in your business once customers see you as a leading authority. Everyone prefers to shop from the best, and this book is your secret to becoming the best.

A solid retailing strategy is key, no matter which segment of apparel retailing you're in. With a well-thought-out approach, as I've used and now share with you, success is within reach. My experiences speak through these pages, ready to guide you.

Trust me—you've got what it takes!

Acknowledgment

A heartfelt thanks to my family and everyone who supports me.

To my parents, you have always believed in me. I'm so grateful for everything you've done.

My wife Madhu, you are not just my partner but the foundation of my strength, I couldn't have done this without your love and patience.

Harsh and Navya, my wonderful children, your laughter and joy infuse my days with purpose and motivation. You inspire me to reach for the stars.

My brother Vikas, your wise advice and support have been my constant companions on this journey. Your friendship means the world to me.

My mentor, Akshar Yadav, your guidance and wisdom have shaped me into the person I am today. I owe much of my success to your invaluable mentorship.

And to all my retailers, you're the reason I wrote this book. Your partnership is so important to me.

Thank you all so much,

Chapter 1

Introduction to the World of Kurtis

Welcome to the vibrant and dynamic world of kurtis! These stylish outfits are now a must-have for modern women, perfect for any occasion. In this section, we'll take a journey into the history of kurtis and discover how they've become a dominant force in the fashion industry. Get ready to explore the fascinating evolution of this beloved garment!

1.1. The Rise of Kurtis in Fashion Retail

Long ago in ancient India, kurtis, also known as kurtas, started their journey. We first hear about them from a very old place called the Indus Valley Civilization. Both men and women wore kurtisback then, usually made from cotton or silk with a simple look.

Wearing a kurti in those times meant you were dressing modestly and purely. It was something you would wear under another layer of clothing that was draped on top. But as time went on, kurtis changed and became something people liked to wear every day. The big change in kurtis happened when the Mughal kings came. They brought a new kind of kurti that was long and baggy with big sleeves and buttons down the front. These kurtis were made of silk or cotton and had beautiful designs inspired by Persian art.

Come the 20th century, kurtis really took off, and everyone started loving them. They weren't just for wearing underneath anymore; they became a way to showcase personal style. Thanks to India's growing cloth-making business, kurtis were everywhere in all kinds of fabrics, patterns, and shapes. Now, people wear them on their own or with tight pants called leggings or with a kind of pants called churidar.

People from India, Bangladesh, Sri Lanka, Nepal, and Pakistan wear them a lot. Even in the United States, people started liking kurtis during the 1960s and '70s.Kurtis are easy to wear for all kinds of things, like hanging out at home or going to parties. They can be simple or fancy, and you don't need lots of decorations on them to look nice. Every part of India has its own special kurti with different colors and patterns. For example, Rajasthani kurtis have block prints and mirrors, while Gujarati ones have shiny zari work.

Kurtis, a traditional Indian garment, has come a long way since its inception. With the evolution of fashion, Kurtis has gone through many modifications in terms of styles, fabrics, and designs. Nowadays, it's a popular choice not only in India but also worldwide. In this blog post, we will take a journey through the evolution of Kurtis, from its roots to modern-day fashion. We will also discuss the different types of Kurtis, their fabrics, designs, and how to style them. So, let's dive in!

Nowadays, in India, girls and women prefer fancy kurtis over western clothes because they're so comfy and pretty. They can wear them to work or parties with some nice earrings and bangles.

So, when girls or women wear a kurti, you are part of a big fashion movement that's all about being comfortable, looking good, and feeling proud of where we come from.

Isn't that amazing? That's the story of how Kurtis rose to be a shining star in the world of fashion retail.

1.2 Types of Kurtis

There are various types of Kurtis available in the market. Here are some of the most popular ones:

- **Anarkali Kurtis:**

  Anarkali Kurtis are long and flowy, with a fitted bodice and a flared skirt. They are inspired by the Mughal era and are perfect for special occasions and weddings.

- **Straight Kurtis:**

  Straight Kurtis are simple and elegant, with a straight cut and a hemline that falls at the knee. They are perfect for daily wear and can be paired with leggings or jeans.

- **A-Line Kurtis:**

  A-Line Kurtis have an A-shaped cut, with a fitted bodice and a flared skirt. They are perfect for all body types and can be worn for both formal and casual occasions.

- **Asymmetric Kurtis:**

Asymmetric Kurtis have an uneven hemline, which adds a unique touch to the garment. They are perfect for those who want to experiment with their look.

- **High-Low Kurtis:**

High-Low Kurtis have a hemline that is shorter in the front and longer at the back. They are perfect for those who want to add a touch of drama to their outfit.

- **Kurta Dupatta Sets:**

Traditional attire consisting of a kurta (a long tunic), paired with a dupatta (a long scarf), offering a blend of modesty, style, and cultural heritage with complimenting bottom (contrast or matching)

- **Cord Sets:**

Matching clothing sets typically consisting of a top and bottoms made from the same fabric or design.

- **Long Gowns:**

Elegant, floor-length dresses often worn for formal occasions or events.

- **Kurta Sharara Set:**

A traditional outfit combining a kurta (a long shirt or tunic) with sharara (wide-legged pants that flare dramatically from the knees).

- **Kurta Skirt Set:**

A set featuring a kurta paired with a skirt, blending traditional style with a touch of modern elegance.

- **Crop Set:**

  A two-piece outfit that includes a cropped top and matching bottoms, ranging from skirts to shorts or pants, often worn in casual or semi-formal settings.

- **Midis:**

  A midi is a type of dress or skirt that falls just below the knee to mid-calf length, blending elegance with casual style.

- **Tunic:**

  A tunic is a loose-fitting garment, usually simple in design, that comes down to the hips or thighs, versatile enough to be worn with leggings, jeans, or as a dress.

- **Dress:**

  A dress is a one-piece garment for women or girls that covers the body and extends down over the legs, varying in length from short to full-length.

- **Gown:**

  A gown is a long elegant dress typically worn for formal occasions, characterised by its full-length skirt and sophisticated design.

- **Short top:**

  A cropped upper garment that ends above or at the midriff, offering a chic and casual look.

- **Shirt top:**

  A versatile top designed like a shirt, often featuring buttons down the front, which can be dressed up or down.

- **Kaftan:**

  A loose, flowing garment with wide sleeves, inspired by traditional Middle Eastern wear, known for its comfort and elegance.

  And so on...

Anarkli kurtis are long and flowy with a fitted bodices and a flared skirts. They are inspired by the mughal era perfect for special occasions and weddings.

Straight kurtis are simple and elegant with a straight cut and a hemline that falls at the knee. They are perfect for daily wear can be paired with legging or jeans.

A -line kurtis have an a shaped cut with a fitted bodice and a flared skirts . They are perfect for all body types and can be worn for both formal and casual occasions.

Asymmetric kurtis have an uneven hemline which adds a unique touch to the garment. They are perfect for those who want to experiment with their look.

High low kurtis have an hemline that is shorter in the front and longer at the back .
They are perfect for those who want to add a touch drama to their outfit .

Kurta dupatta sets – traditional attire consisting of a kurta [A long tunic], paired with
a dupatta [A long scarf], offering a blend of modesty , style , and cultural heritage
with complimenting bottom [contrast or matching].

<u>Cord-sets</u> matching clothing sets typically consisting of a top and bottoms made from the same fabric or design.

<u>Long gowns</u> – elegant , floor - length dresses often worn for formal occasions or events. .

Kurta sharara set – A traditional outfit combining a kurta [a long shirt or tunic] with a sharara [wide-legged pants that flare dramatically from the knees] .

[

Kurta skirt set – A set featuring a kurta paired with a skirt , blending traditional style with a touch of modern elegance .

<u>Crop</u> <u>set</u> – A two-piece outfit that includes a cropped top and matching bottoms, ranging from skirts to shorts or pants, often worn in casual or semi-formal settings.

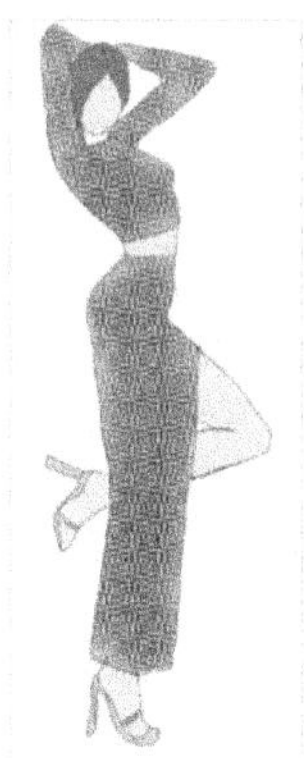

<u>Midis</u> – A midi is a type of dress or skirt that falls just below the knee to mid-calf length, blending elegance with casual style .

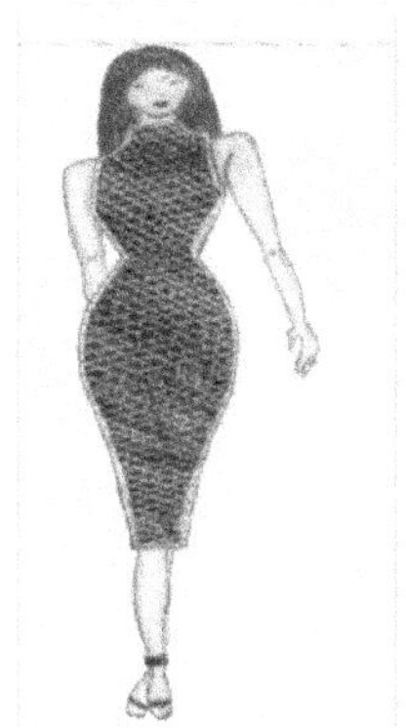

<u>Tunics-</u> A tunic is a loose fitting garment, usually simple in design, that comes down to the hips or thighs, versatile enough to be worn with leggings, jeans or as a dress.

<u>Dress</u> – A dress is a one piece garment for women or girls that covers the body and extends down over the legs, varying in length from short to full length.

<u>Gown</u> – A gown is a long elegant dress typically worn for formal occasions, characterized by its full-length skirt and sophisticated design.

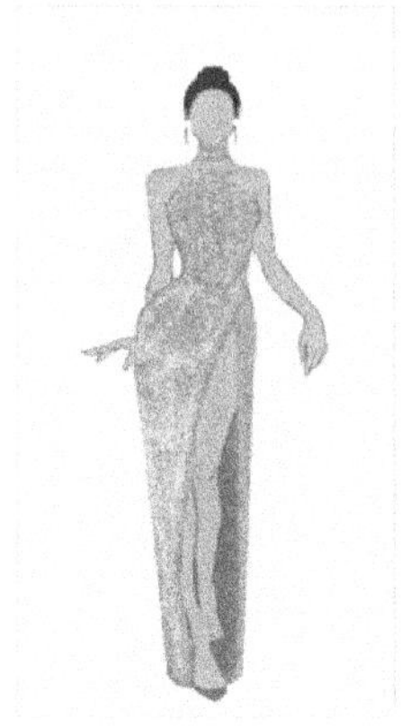 

<u>Short</u> <u>top</u> – A crop top is type of shirt that is characterized by its shorter length, typically ending above the waistline or just below the bust. They comes in various styles, from casual and sophisticated, making them versatile for different occasions.

<u>Shirt Top</u> – An apparel meant for upper part of the body worn over the pants having front opening with facility of buttoning which is used as formal and casual wear.

1.3 Fabrics Used in Kurtis

Kurtis come in various fabrics, each with its own unique properties. Here are some of the most commonly used fabrics in Kurtis:

- **Cotton:** Cotton is a lightweight, breathable fabric that is perfect for summer wear.

- **Rayon:** Rayon, also known as viscose and commercialised in some countries as sabra silk or cactus silk, is a semi-synthetic fibre made from natural sources of regenerated cellulose, such as wood and related agricultural products.

- **Silk:** Silk is a luxurious fabric that is often used for formal occasions.

- **Chiffon:** Chiffon,a delicate and sheer fabric,is commonly used for the sleeves or dupatta of a kurti.

- **Georgette:** Georgette,prized for its lightweight and flowing nature, is a popular choice for the main body of a kurti.

- **Crepe:** Crepe with its lightweight and wrinkle-resistant properties, is favored for casual kurtis.

- **Modal:** Modal is a soft, smooth, and breathable fabric made from beechwood fiber, known for its durability and comfort, often used in activewear and intimate garments.

- **Muslin (Muzlin):** Muslin is a lightweight, finely woven, breathable fabric known for its softness, making it ideal for summer clothing and traditionally used for making patterns in garment design.

This is Indian kurti's long and fascinating history. It started as a simple and useful outfit for regular wear, but over the years, it became a symbol of fashion and culture in India. The kurti has a long history filled with different styles, influences, and changes, but it's still loved for its flexibility and classic look.

1.4 Understanding the Kurti Craze: From Traditional to Trendy

As I said, kurti is a really popular dress that lots of girls and women in India wear. It started as a simple, comfy dress that women wore every day, made to help them stay cool and move around easily.

Many places in India made the kurti in a special way, using different kinds of cloth and designs. This made every kurti special, showing its traditional roots. Then, as more people around the world started sharing their fashion styles, the kurti began to change. Designers made them shorter or longer, changed the sleeves, and used new kinds of cloth that weren't used before. This made the kurti really fashionable and cool, and not just something you would wear every day.

People from other countries started to like kurtis too. They saw how pretty and easy to wear they were and began to wear them with jeans or skirts, or even as dresses. So, the kurti became famous all over the world, not just in India

Movies and TV shows helped make kurtis really popular. When famous actresses wore kurtis, everyone wanted to have one. Now, you could see kurtis being worn by all kinds of people, not just in cities but in the countryside too.

Today, you can find kurtis everywhere, from fancy stores to small shops in the market. They come in old-fashioned styles with cool designs and patterns that have been used for a long time. But now, they also have new, fun designs that younger people like a lot. Because so many people want to buy kurtis, they help a lot of people have jobs, like those who make them and sell them. The kurti has become a big deal in the clothing business and helps a lot of people earn money.

Everyone loves kurtis today because they are comfy, stylish, and keep changing to be new and exciting, but still remember the old ways. Whether someone likes an old-style kurti or a new one with fun designs, kurtis are loved by people not just in India, but all around the world now.

Chapter 2

The Right Strategies for Your Store

Alright! First, give yourself a pat on the back because you are part of a business with a very proud history. Well done on that!

Now, let's get going. Sometimes we overlook things, don't we? Like, when we start a business with lots of excitement, but then, if we don't get the results we wanted, it can start to feel not so fun anymore. It might even feel like no matter how hard we work, we're just not getting what we hoped for.

After my last book, "The Future of Women's Wear Retailing," I got to meet lots of store owners and did a bunch of research. That's when I decided that my next book would be about strategies and techniques that actually work and deliver results.

In the upcoming sections, you're going to find all those action points to follow, and I promise, if you stick to them, you'll start seeing the results you want. I'm telling you this from my own experience. So, get ready to be inspired and work towards the success you deserve!

2.1. Knowing Your Customer Base

So, first things first, it's important to really understand your customers and what they like. It might seem easy, but it's not always so simple. Today, the women's wear retail stores that are doing really well are the ones that have figured this out.

You need to be clear about who your customers are and what they really want, what they dream of having. When you do this, you'll only buy the garments that you know will sell quickly in your store. You shouldn't just pick out designs first and then try to find customers for them.

In simple words, know your friends – I mean, customers – like you know your favorite game. When you know what they like and what they wish for, you can pick the best dresses that they will love and buy fast! Remember, in your store, make sure you have the garments that your customers are looking for, just like having the right pieces to win a board game. That's the way to win in this business!

Let's talk about a shop called "Dress Corner," owned by a friendly lady named Aisha. Aisha's shop is special because she really knows what her customers like. She spends time chatting with them and learns about their lives and what they enjoy wearing. For instance, Aisha found out that her customers were looking for dresses that are perfect for going on vacation and for relaxing weekends at home. With this in mind, she brought in a selection of vibrant and comfortable kurtis, perfect for a beach getaway or a family picnic. These kurtis became an instant favorite, and soon enough, "Dress Corner" was the go-to place for vacation wear. Aisha's success came from her keen understanding of her customers' needs and making sure she had just the right clothes for them.

Humne kya sikha? (What did we learn?)

Customers *se dosti karni hai* (Make friends with your customers), then they will let you know about their needs and desires.

2.2. The Importance of Fabric and Quality

Choosing the right fabric and ensuring its quality is very important when selecting the designs for your store. It's something you can't ignore. I have seen many stores that didn't do well because their fabric and its quality weren't good—almost 31% of them had this problem. I'm not telling you this because it's a new idea or something store owners don't know, but there's a big difference between knowing something and really paying attention to it. Even when they know better, some store owners pick lower quality fabric because it's cheaper or on discount. Which is a very sad thing to do. Remember, good quality sells itself, sells over and over again, while poor quality is hard to sell even once.

Once there was a store called "Sunny Fabrics" in a small town. The owner, Mr. Kumar, was a kind man who loved garments. When he first opened his shop, he wanted to save money, so he bought cheaper fabrics that were not very good quality. He thought this was a smart move because he got discounts. However,customers didn't return after their first purchase. They didn't like how the clothes felt and how quickly they wore out.

Mr. Kumar noticed another store, "Lasting Impressions," always seemed busy. This store only sold garments made of really nice fabric that felt good to wear. The owner, Mrs. Shah, might have spent more on her fabrics, but her customers kept coming back for more because they loved what they bought.

So, Mr. Kumar decided to change. He started to choose better fabrics, even though they cost more. Soon, his store became just as busy as Mrs. Shah's. Customers in town started talking about how great the clothes from "Sunny Fabrics" were. Now, Mr. Kumar's store is a big success. He learned that selling good quality means people will want to buy again and again, while poor quality might save money at first but won't make customers happy or loyal.

Chapter 3

Design Elements That Drive Sales

When you're choosing Kurtis to sell in your store, think about what makes a picture beautiful. Is it the colours, the shapes, or maybe the story it tells? Just like a great picture, the right Kurtis can make your store stand out. Let's see how!

3.1. Colour Role in Kurti Selection

- **Bright and Happy:**

  Colours can make someone feel happy or calm. Think about what colours your customers like. Do they enjoy bright colours like the sun or soft colours like the sky? Offering a variety of colors ensures there's something for everyone's taste and mood.

- **Seasons Matter:**

  In summer, light colours keep us cool, and in winter, dark colours make us feel warm. Choose colours that fit the season and evoke the right mood for your customers. Additionally, consider seasonal trends to stay relevant and attract shoppers seeking the latest styles.

3.2. Patterns, Prints, and Embroidery: What Sells More?

- **Tell a Story:**

  Patterns and prints are like stories on fabric. Some tell tales of forests and rivers, while others show off beautiful flowers or animals. Understanding the stories your customers are drawn to can help you select Kurtis that resonate with them on a personal level and create a connection with your brand.

- **Special Touch:**

  Embroidery is like the icing on a cake. It makes a simple Kurti look special. Find out what embroidery your customers think is pretty and pay attention to the small details that can make a big difference in their purchasing decisions. Providing unique embellishments sets your Kurtis apart from the rest.

3.3. Cuts and Styles: A Fitting Choice for Your Market

- **Shape and Size:**

  Just like people, Kurtis come in all shapes and sizes. Some are long, and some are short. Choose the ones that fit your customers best by offering a range of sizes and styles to accommodate diverse body types and preferences. Ensuring inclusivity in your selection fosters a welcoming shopping experience for all.

- **Comfort is Key:**

A Kurti might look nice, but if it's not comfy, people won't wear it. Make sure the Kurtis you pick are cozy by selecting soft fabrics and designs that allow for ease of movement. Prioritizing comfort ensures satisfied customers who are likely to return for more and spread positive word-of-mouth about your store.

3.4 Current Trends vs. Classic Styles

- **What's New:**

Keep an eye on what's trendy. Maybe it's a new color or a type of collar that's in style. Make sure you have room for new trends by keeping your collection up-to-date with the latest fashion styles. This shows that your store is dedicated to providing cool and new choices for customers who love fashion.

- **Timeless Beauty:**

Classic styles never get old. Some customers always look for these, so have some classic Kurtis too. When you offer clothes that never go out of style along with the latest trendy ones, you attract more kinds of customers. This way, everyone can find something they like, whether they're into what's new or they prefer something that always looks good. Having classic styles also makes your shop feel fancier and more timeless.

Remember, selling Kurtis isn't just about having a large inventory of them. It's about having the right ones that make your customers feel good when they wear them. Think about what they like, what makes them comfortable, and what makes them say "wow"! That's how you choose Kurtis that not only sell quickly but also leave your customers delighted and eager o return for more.

Chapter 4

Sourcing Strategies for Retailers

Finding the right Kurtis for your store is like going on a treasure hunt. You need to know where to look and who can help you find the treasures! Let's learn how to work with people who make Kurtis and pick tphe best ones for every season.

4.1. Establishing Relationships with Suppliers

- **Make Friendship with the suppliers:**

  Think of your suppliers as friends. When you have a good friendship, they will always want to give you their best Kurtis. Talk to them, understand how they make Kurtis, and share what your customers like. Building a strong relationship with suppliers ensures mutual trust and better cooperation, leading to more exclusive deals and priority access to new designs.

- **Visit Them:**

  If you can, visit suppliers frequently. Seeing how you can help you choose better and might even get you better prices. Visiting their workshops or factories allows you to understand their production process and quality standards firsothand, fostering transparency and facilitating smoother collaborations.

- **Talk Often:**

  Keep in touch with your suppliers. Call or message them to know what's new and tell them what your customers are asking for. This way, they'll think of you first when they have something special. Regular communication helps you stay updated on new arrivals and enables you to provide feedback on customer preferences, strengthening your partnership with suppliers.

4.2 The Significance of Seasonal Selection

- **Match the Weather:**

  Just like we wear hats in the sun and coats in the cold, Kurtis also change with the weather. Pick light and breezy Kurtis for summer and warm and cozy ones for winter. This way, your customers will find what they need all year round. Adapting your collection to match seasonal trends ensures that your customers stay comfortable and stylish regardless of the weather, enhancing their overall shopping experience.

- **Festival and Vacations outfits:**

  Some Kurtis are perfect for special times of the year like festivals or vacations. Keep track of these special times and have the right Kurtis ready. Your customers will be happy to find the perfect Kurti for every occasion at your store. Offering curated selections for festive seasons and holidays enhances the shopping experience and encourages repeat visits, fostering customer loyalty.

- **Be Ahead of the Season:**

  Start thinking about the next season a little early. If you have summer Kurtis ready when the first warm breeze blows, everyone will come to your store first! Anticipating seasonal trends and stocking up early ensures that you're prepared to meet customer demand before competitors, giving your store a competitive edge and establishing it as a trendsetter in the market.

By making good friends with the people who make Kurtis and choosing them carefully for each season, your store will always have the best selection. Your customers will love that they can always find something perfect to wear, no matter the time of year! With a friendly atmosphere and a knack for picking the right Kurtis, your store becomes a go-to destination for stylish and comfortable fashion.

Chapter 5

The Pricing Puzzle: What to Consider

5.1. Competitive Pricing Strategies

Imagine you're playing a game where you have to price a product. If you set the price too high, your friends might not buy it. But if it's too low, you might not have enough money to buy more lemons. The trick is to look at what others are charging for their products, find the gap, and set your price so that your customers still buy from you, and you can still get more. This is called strategic pricing. It means making your Kurtis affordable but also making sure you can keep your shop running.

5.2. Pricing Points and Customer Perception

Now, think about when you choose a gift. If you find two gifts that look the same but one is more expensive, you might think it's better. Customers think like this too. If your kurtis are priced too low, people might think they're not of good quality. But if they're priced just right, people will think they're getting something special. This is about finding the perfect price that makes your customers feel they're getting a great deal for something really nice.

5.3. Price vs Value

So, the big idea is how customers see the value of an outfit compared to its price. Value can be something you can see and touch, like how pretty the fabric is, or something you can't see, like feeling special when you wear it. We always need to make sure we're giving more value than what we're asking for in price. If we do that, then customers won't mind the price. Usually, when people talk a lot about the price, it's because they don't see the value or think the value isn't enough for the price.

Simple Example: Price vs. Value - The Magic Jacket

- **Visible Value:**

    Imagine you're buying a jacket. This jacket is not just any jacket; it looks amazing with bright colours and has lots of pockets, which is pretty handy. That's the visible value - what makes this jacket not just good but great in how it looks and works.

- **Invisible Value:**

    Now, imagine this jacket is also known as the "Magic Jacket" in your school. Everyone who wears this jacket feels like a superhero. It makes you feel brave and confident, even on days when you have a big test. That feeling, that's the invisible value. You can't see it, but it's definitely there.

Conclusion

The jacket costs a bit more than other jackets. But because it makes you look cool and feel like a superhero, you and your friends think it's totally worth it. The price doesn't feel so high anymore because the jacket gives you so much more in return - both in looking awesome and feeling great.

So, when you choose something to buy, think about what it gives you, not just in how it looks, but also in how it makes you feel. That's how you know you're getting something really valuable, no matter the price.

Price to Value Ratio

Always remember: Customers do not buy the best; they do not buy the best features they understand best. So, always keep in mind how we can best explain the value to our customers. By playing the pricing vs. value proposition game well, you'll have happy customers and a happy kurti shop!

Let's get clarity with this small story:

Once upon a time, two friends, Akash and Sunil, decided to open a lemonade stand. Akash wanted to sell their lemonade cheaply so that everyone would buy it. Sunil thought that if they made the lemonade extra tasty and used fancy cups, they could charge a little more. (These are all visible & invisible values). They tried Akash's way first but didn't make enough money to buy more supplies. Then they tried Sunil's way. They added fresh lemons and mint and used colourful straws and cups. They put up a sign that said, "The Best Lemonade in Town!"

People loved the lemonade and didn't mind paying more because it made them feel happy and refreshed. Akash and Sunil learned that it's not just about how much lemonade costs, but how it makes their customers feel. They made enough money to keep their stand running all summer and even had some left over to buy a new game they wanted.

This story shows us that when you give something special to your customers, like the best lemonade or the prettiest Kurti, they will be happy to pay a price that makes everyone feel good.

Chapter 6

Adapting to Change: Keeping Up with Kurti Trends

Fashion is like the seasons; it keeps changing. To make your store the best place for Kurtis, you need to become a fashion detective and listen to what your customers love. Let's explore how!

6.1 The Power of Fashion Forecasting

Imagine you have a magic crystal ball that can show you what Kurtis everyone will want next month or next year. That's what fashion forecasting is like! It helps you know what colors, styles, and patterns will be popular so you can have them in your store before anyone else.

- **Look Around:**

  Pay attention to what people wear in movies, on TV shows, and in magazines. These are clues to the next big thing in Kurti fashion. Additionally, observe what influencers and celebrities are wearing as they often set trends.

- **Listen to the Experts:**

  There are fashion experts who study trends and make predictions. Following their advice can be like having a treasure map to the most wanted Kurtis. Consider subscribing to fashion magazines, attending industry events, or following reputable fashion blogs for insights.

- **Trendsetting Supplier Partnerships:**

  Partner with suppliers who always introduce trending and innovative concepts. Such suppliers are a gold mine for you. Collaborating with suppliers who have a keen eye for upcoming trends ensures that your store remains ahead of the curve in offering the latest and most sought-after Kurtis.

6.2 Incorporating Customer Suggestions into Inventory Selection

Your customers are your best advisors. They can tell you what they want to wear, which is like having secret codes to what will sell the best.

- **Ask and Listen:**

  Whenever customers come to your store, ask them what they wish they could find. Maybe they want Kurtis with pockets or in a special colour. Write down their ideas and look for those Kurtis. Engaging with customers through conversation helps you understand their preferences better and tailor your inventory accordingly.

- **Feedback Box:**

  Put a box in your store where customers can drop their suggestions. It's a fun way for them to tell you what they're looking for, and it's like getting a list of treasures to find for your store. Providing a platform for customers to share their opinions encourages active participation and fosters a sense of ownership among them in shaping the offerings of your store.

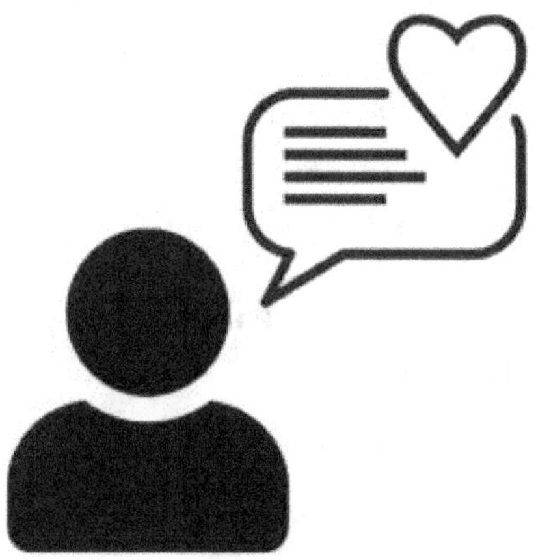

A Simple Story: "The Trendy Kurti Store"

There was once a store called "Kurti Magic" that was run by a smart retailer named Arjun. Arjun loved his store, but noticed that not as many people were coming in to shop. He wanted to find a way to make his store everyone's favourite.

Arjun started watching fashion shows and reading fashion magazines to see which kurtis might become popular. He also placed a big, colourful box in his store labelled "Your Fashion Wishes." Customers loved dropping their suggestions into the box, and Arjun enjoyed reading them.

Using what he learned from the fashion forecasts and his customers' wishes, Arjun filled his store with the latest trends and the exact styles his customers wanted. Soon, his store was full of happy shoppers excited to find kurtis that were just right for them.

Arjun's store became the most popular kurti store in town, all because he learned to follow the trends and listen to his customers. Arjun showed that with a little bit of detective work and a lot of listening, any store can become a treasure chest of the latest and most loved kurtis.

Remember, keeping up with fashion trends and listening to your customers can turn your store into a magical place where everyone finds something they love.

Chapter 7

Beyond the Basics:
Expanding Your Kurti Range

Imagine your store as a huge box of crayons with all kinds of colours. Now, think about how you can make your box even more special with colours nobody else has. That's what we're going to do with your kurti collection!

7.1 Introducing Plus Sizes and other Concepts

Think about when everyone in class gets a chance to play a game, no matter if they're tall, short, big, or small. That's how we want everyone to feel when they come to your store.

- **Plus Sizes:**

    Just like every student in class is unique, every customer is different. By having kurtis in plus sizes, you're making sure that everyone finds a kurti that fits them perfectly, just like every student finds a spot in the game. Offering plus sizes ensures inclusivity and caters to a diverse range of body types.

- **Other Concepts:**

    Imagine having kurtis that are perfect for different activities, like a kurti you can wear as lounge wear or one that's comfy for reading in class. This means everyone can find a kurti for whatever they love doing. Providing versatile options for various occasions enhances the shopping experience and meets the diverse needs of your customers.

7.2 Exploring Fusion Wear: Blending Tradition with Modernity

Now, imagine mixing paint to create a new colour. That's what fusion wear does with kurtis. It mixes traditional designs with modern styles to create something totally new and exciting.

- **Blending Styles:**

  Imagine a kurti that has cool, modern pockets for your gadgets but also beautiful, traditional patterns. It's like having the best of both worlds, where you honour the past but also embrace today's fun trends. Fusion wear offers a unique and contemporary twist to traditional attire, appealing to customers who appreciate a blend of heritage and modernity.

- **Traditional Prints in Modern Clothes:**

  Discover how fusion wear uses prints from different cultures, like tie-dye or block prints, on modern Kurtis. It's like bringing old designs into the present, making them feel fresh and exciting. This mix of cultures adds a special touch to the clothes we wear, showing off our heritage in a modern way.

Making Your Store a Magical Place

By adding these new kinds of kurtis to your store, you're turning it into a magical crayon box where everyone finds their perfect colour. Remember, the more options you have, the more people you'll make happy. So, let's get creative and fill your store with all these wonderful kurtis!

Chapter 8

Stock Management

Imagine your store is like a cookie jar. You want it filled with the tastiest cookies, but you also don't want cookies from last month sitting at the bottom, right? Let's make sure your kurtis are always as fresh and exciting as newly baked cookies!

8.1. Inventory Management: The Key to Fresh Collections

Imagine your store's kurtis are like a bunch of different flowers in a garden. Just like you need to take care of flowers, you also need to take care of your kurtis. You have to know which kurtis are like the bright sunflowers that everyone notices and which are like the daisies waiting for their turn to shine.

- **Keep It Fresh:**

  Always know what kurtis you have and how long they've been sitting in your store. It's like looking after your garden, making sure all the flowers get enough sunlight and water to stay beautiful and fresh. This way, every time someone visits your store, they see something new and pretty, just like a garden that's always blooming.

8.2. Stock Balancing: The Art of Right Quantity

Having the right amount of kurtis is very important. It's like making sure your garden gets just the right amount of rain—not too much that the plants drown and not too little that they dry out.

- **Just Enough:**

    Imagine if you baked cookies and made too many. Not all of them would get eaten, right? But if you made too few, some of your friends might not get any. That's how it is with your kurtis. If you have too many of one kind, you might not be able to sell them all. But if you have too few, you might not have enough for everyone who wants to buy them. So, try to have just the right number of kurtis in your store, so every customer finds their "cookie" and there are no cookies going stale.

Keeping Your Store Just Right

Think of your store as the best cookie jar in town. You want it to be full of the yummiest, freshest cookies. When friends come over, you want them to find their favourite cookie, try some new flavours, and always leave happy, knowing they want to come back for more.

Your kurtis are like those cookies. You want to have the newest styles and the right amount, so everyone finds something they love. And just like a cookie jar that always has something sweet, your store will always have something beautiful. Let's make sure your store is the place everyone wants to visit, just like everyone loves visiting the kitchen when they know there's a jar full of cookies waiting!

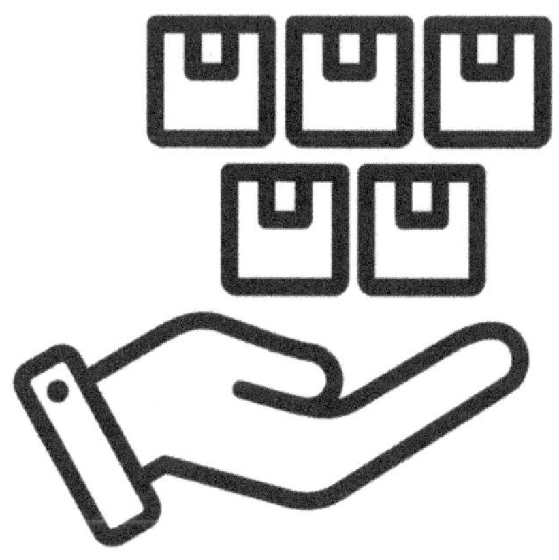

Buy Right Quantity

Chapter 9

Case Studies: What Worked for Successful Kurti Retailers

Here are some stories to inspire you and show you what you can achieve in your store. Let these success stories spark your imagination and guide you to unlock the full potential of your retail space. Discover how embracing change, listening to customer feedback, and innovating your offerings can transform your store into a thriving hub of fashion and community. Whether it's trying new online strategies, crafting unique in-store experiences, or supporting local craftsmanship, there's a wealth of ideas waiting to be explored. Let these narratives inspire you to take bold steps, carve your niche, and write your own success story.

9.1 Retailer Spotlights: Strategies That Led to Increased Sales

Case Study 1: The Social Meidia Star

Once upon a time, there was a kurti store called "Colorful Kurtis." The owner, Aarav, was looking for ways to attract more customers. He decided to use social media to showcase his beautiful kurtis. He posted pictures of the kurtis with fun facts about the designs and fabrics. People loved it! They shared the posts with friends, and soon, more and more people came to buy kurtis from Aarav's store. His secret? Sharing the beauty and stories behind each kurti, making everyone feel connected and excited to visit his store.

Case Study 2: The Customer's Choice Corner

Another store, "Kurti Junction," run by Meera, wasn't selling many kurtis. Meera then came up with a brilliant idea. She asked her customers what kinds of kurtis they wanted to see in her store. She made a special corner in her store called "The Customer's Choice" filled with kurtis picked by her customers. This made her customers feel special, and they told their friends about how Meera's store made their wishes come true. Sales went up, and "Kurti Junction" became a happy place full of customers' favourite kurtis.

Case Study 3: The Trendsetter

Riya used to feel sad because her boutique didn't sell many clothes, and she thought about closing it. But one day, she met Naveen at an event, introduced by a friend. She talked to Naveen about her problems, and then he decided to help her find solutions. He explained some modern techniques to come out of it. And after that, Riya's Boutique always had new clothes. Every month, Riya brought in new collections based on themes like festivals, seasons, or popular colors. Her secret? She stayed updated by watching fashion shows and learning about new trends.

Case Study 4: The Personal Touch

Karan used to feel really upset because he had a lot of debt and couldn't pay his employees. He even felt like he might want to end his life. Then, one of his workers suggested he read a book by Naveen and meet him. Somehow, Karan managed to meet Naveen and asked for his help. Naveen, always ready to help, taught Karan importance of personal touch. After that, Karan's Kurti Corner, started offering a special service. Customers could now get small changes made to their clothes right there in the store. Adding a pocket or adjusting the length made customers really happy because it showed that their needs were important.

Case Study 5: The Storyteller

When Anita started her kurti business, she lacked knowledge about business and trends. Initially, she sold regular kurtis, which kept her shop running but didn't lead to any growth. She was very worried about how to expand her business. Then, one of her friends told her about Mr. Naveen and suggested meeting him for help. With her friend's assistance, she managed to meet him. Since then, Anita's Ethnic Wear didn't just sell kurtis; it sold stories. Each tag had a little story about the craft or the artisan who made it. This storytelling made customers feel connected to the culture and the people behind the kurtis.

Case Study 6: The Online Star

Vikram ran a small kurti store for several years, but during the COVID-19 pandemic, he had to close it down. He found himself struggling to make ends meet alone at home. The closure of his shop caused him a lot of distress, and he couldn't figure out how to sustain himself. That's when he started reading books to understand online business. By chance, he came across a book by Mr. Naveen, which he read and understood. He realized that in today's world, people prefer to have everything delivered to their homes and shop online. Understanding this, he also decided to list his shop on online platforms, which proved to be very beneficial. Vikram's Virtual Kurti Shop became an online-only store. He used engaging videos to showcase how the kurtis looked from different angles and on different body types. His engaging content and honest reviews built trust and boosted sales.

Case Study 7: The Community Leader

Deepa's store "Sew in Style" was doing quite well, but she noticed that her customers were not returning as frequently. Gradually, she was losing her trusted and loyal customers because the market competition had increased significantly. Then, during a fashion event in Mumbai, she met Mr. Naveen, who gave her some unique business ideas. One of these ideas was to host monthly fashion shows in her store, using real customers as models. This community involvement made her customers feel like part of Deepa's family, turning them into loyal fans and brand ambassadors for Deepa's Designs.

9.2 From Flop to Top: Turnaround Stories

Case Study 8: The Discount Days

"Sunshine Kurtis" was a small store that was almost about to close because not many people were coming in. The owner, Nikhil, decided to try something new. He introduced "Discount Days" once a month, where all kurtis werep[;'\u sold at a special price. He also made sure that every "Discount Day" had different kurtis on sale to keep things exciting. Word spread about these special days, and his store was packed with customers looking forward to the surprises Nikhil had in store for them. Nikhil's store went from almost closing to being the talk of the town!

Case Study 9: The Eco-Friendly Fashion

Sara's store, "Green Kurtis," was struggling because it looked just like any other kurti store. Sara decided to make her store stand out by only selling eco-friendly kurtis. She used social media to teach people about the benefits of eco-friendly fashion and decorated her store with plants and recycled materials. Soon, her store attracted customers who cared about the environment and wanted to support a business that shared their values. "Green Kurtis" became a special place where fashion met caring for the planet, and Sara's sales soared.

Case Study 10: The Big Pivot

Neha's Niche was struggling until she decided to focus solely on sustainable and organic kurtis. This niche market was untapped, and her commitment to the environment turned her store from a flop to a top destination for eco-conscious shoppers.

Neha's Niche carved out a special place in the market by embracing sustainability. Her decision to stock exclusively sustainable and organic kurtis not only set her apart but also established her store as a pioneer in eco-friendly fashion. This bold move resonated with a growing base of environmentally aware customers, propelling her store to new heights.

Case Study 11: The Feedback Loop

Aman's Apparel was once barely making sales. Aman started actively asking for and listening to customer feedback, then quickly implemented the suggestions. This responsiveness to customer needs transformed his store into a thriving business.

Aman turned his store around by placing customer feedback at the heart of his business strategy. This open dialogue and quick adaptation showcased his commitment to customer satisfaction, fostering a loyal community that viewed Aman's Apparel not just as a store, but as a brand that listens and evolves with its patrons.

Case Study 12: The Value Add

p[;'\/Priya's Place was just another kurti store until she began offering free style consultations. Customers loved the personalised advice, and Priya's Place became known as the go-to for not just kurtis but fashion guidance, significantly increasing sales.

At Priya's Place, the introduction of free style consultations provided an unmatched shopping experience, transforming casual browsers into loyal customers. This added service, emphasising personalization and care, highlighted Priya's dedication to helping each customer find their perfect style match.

Case Study 13: The Tech Turnaround

Sanjay's Kurti Spot was old-fashioned until Sanjay introduced an app for virtual try-ons. This tech innovation attracted a younger crowd and gave the store a much-needed boost, making it a popular spot for tech-savvy shoppers.

Sanjay's integration of technology into his traditional business model brought a refreshing change to the shopping experience. The launch of a virtual try-on app was a game-changer, appealing to the modern, tech-oriented consumer and breathing new life into Sanjay's Kurti Spot with a blend of innovation and tradition.

Case Study 14: The Local Love

Manav's Market was nearly shutting down until he made a smart move: sourcing all his kurtis from local artisans, highlighting their talent. Suddenly, his store became a community favorite, praised for backing local artistry, and saw a remarkable turnaround.

By exclusively sourcing from local artisans, Manav infused his store with authenticity and a special local touch. This emphasis on local craftsmanship not only rescued his business but also made Manav's Market a vital part of the community, honoring the richness of local traditions and boosting the local economy.

Lessons Learned

These stories show us that with a little creativity and by listening to what customers want, any kurti retailer can turn their store into a success story. Whether it's through using social media, letting customers choose, having special sale days, or standing for a cause, the key is to connect with people and make them excited to shop from you. Let's take inspiration from these stories and think of new ways to make our kurti stores flourish!

Chapter 10

The Checklist for Kurti Retail Excellence

Running a kurti store is like being the captain of a ship. You need to know where you're going, how to get there, and make sure everyone on board is happy. This chapter is your map and compass to help you sail smoothly!

10.1. Quick Reference Guide for Kurti Buying

Imagine you have a magic book that tells you exactly what to buy for your store. That's what this guide is like! Here are a few tips:

- **Know What's Popular:**

  Keep an eye on what types of kurtis everyone is wearing. Is it floral prints or geometric patterns? Long sleeves or sleeveless? This helps you pick the right styles.

- **Quality Matters:**

  Just like you wouldn't want a toy that breaks easily, make sure the kurtis you choose are well-made and will last. Check for stitching quality, fabric durability, and overall craftsmanship to ensure customer satisfaction.

- **Price Right:**

  Think about how much you would want to spend on a new toy. Price your kurtis so that your customers feel they're getting good value for their money. Conduct market research to understand pricing trends and set competitive yet profitable prices for your products.

10.2. Seasonal Buying Guide

Buying kurtis for your store is like picking outfits for a year-round vacation. You need different things for summer than you do for winter!

- **Summer:**

  Look for light, airy fabrics and bright colours. Consider adding sleeveless or short-sleeved options to your collection to provide relief from the heat while keeping customers stylishly comfortable.

- **Winter:**

  Choose kurtis in thicker fabrics and darker colours to keep your customers cosy. Explore options with added layers or insulation to offer warmth without compromising on style during the colder months.

- **Festials:**

  Remember special times of the year and have kurtis that match these occasions, like sparkly ones for Diwali or elegant ones for Eid. Collaborate with local designers or artisans to offer unique, festive designs that resonate with your customers' cultural celebrations.

10.3. Final Thoughts: Building a Brand, Not Just a Business

Imagine your store is not just a place to buy kurtis but a favourite hangout spot for your customers. Here's how to make that happen:

- **Be Friendly:**

  Always greet your customers with a smile, just like you would welcome friends into your home. Engage them in conversation, ask about their day, and create a warm atmosphere that encourages them to linger and explore.

- **Listen and Learn:**

  Pay attention to what your customers like and don't like. This helps you know them better and make your store their go-to place.

- **Stand Out:**

  Think about what makes your store special. Maybe it's your amazing collection of kurtis or your super fun sales events. Use what makes you unique to build a brand that people love and remember.

Running a successful kurti store is about more than just selling clothes. It's about creating a place where customers feel valued and excited to come back. Use this checklist to make your store the best it can be, and watch how your happy customers help your store grow!

Retailer's Checklist for Kurti Excellence

Understanding the World of Kurtis

- Research the history and current trends in kurti fashion.
- Stay updated with global and local fashion trends.

The Right Strategies for Your Store

- Identify your target customer demographic.
- Ensure your collection caters to the tastes and needs of your target market.

Design Elements That Drive Sales

- Select a diverse range of colours that appeal to your customer base.
- Include a variety of patterns, prints, and embroidery styles in your inventory.
- Keep a balance between traditional cuts and contemporary styles.
- Regularly update your collection with current trends without neglecting classic styles.

Sourcing Strategies

- Build strong relationships with suppliers known for quality and innovation.
- Incorporate seasonal selections to keep your inventory fresh and relevant.

Pricing Strategies

- Develop competitive pricing strategies that offer value for money.

- Understand and apply pricing points that align with customer perception.

- Balance price and value to ensure customer satisfaction and repeat business.

Adapting to Change

- Use fashion forecasting to stay ahead of trends.

- Actively incorporate customer feedback into inventory decisions.

Expanding Your Kurti Range

- Introduce plus sizes and maternity wear to cater to all customers.

- Collaborate with local designers for exclusive lines.

- Explore fusion wear, blending traditional and modern elements.

Stock Management

- Implement an effective inventory management system.

- Practice stock balancing to avoid overstocking or stockouts.

Building a Brand

- Focus on creating a unique brand experience, not just a business.

- Prioritise customer service to build loyalty.

- Engage in community and social media to enhance your brand presence.

Final Thoughts

- Regularly review and adapt business strategies based on market feedback.

- Continuously seek ways to innovate and differentiate your store from competitors.

- Commit to ethical practices and sustainability in your sourcing and business operations.

This checklist serves as a roadmap for kurti retailers aiming for success in a competitive market. By methodically addressing each point, you can build a thriving business that not only sells kurtis but also builds lasting relationships with customers.

Further Steps

Once you've got the hang of picking the right kurtis that sell quickly, just like we talked about in this book, there's more you can do! You can get in touch to learn how to use the science of marketing to boost your sales even higher, become a well-known brand, attract even more customers, and become the number one retailer in your area.

Boosting Sales with Marketing

- **Learn About Marketing:**

  Marketing is like telling a story about your kurtis that makes everyone want to listen. We can show you how to tell that story in a way that gets more people to come to your store. Additionally, we'll explore various marketing channels such as social media, email campaigns, and influencer collaborations to expand your reach and attract new customers.

Becoming a Brand

- **Be a Brand Everyone Knows:**

  Just like everyone has a favourite ice cream flavour, you want everyone to have your store as their favourite place to shop. We'll talk about how to be that favourite by making your store and your kurtis something special that everyone talks about. Moreover, we'll dig deeper into branding tactics that include how your store looks, what you say about your brand, and how customers feel when they shop with you. This helps create a strong and unforgettable brand image that people recognize and remember.

Attracting More Customers

- **Getting More Friends to Play:**

  Imagine if you had the coolest playground. We'll share tips on how to make your store like that playground where everyone wants to come, look around, and buy your kurtis. Additionally, we'll talk about ways to connect with your community, like organizing events or workshops. This helps create a sense of belonging around your store and brings in more customers through recommendations from others.

Being Number One in Your Area

- **Be the Leader of the Pack:**

  Just like being the captain of a team, we'll help you learn ways to lead the pack in your area. This means having the best kurtis, the best prices, and the best shopping experience that makes you the go-to store for everyone. Furthermore, we'll explore innovative strategies to stay ahead of the competition and maintain your leadership position in the market.

So, if you're ready to take these next steps and make your store the place everyone talks about, let's get started. Together, we'll make sure your store isn't just a store, but a favorite shopping destination for all!

Let's Connect!!!

Ready to make your store the best it can be? Reach out to me at: **nb@mnfashions.com**

Together, we'll make your dream store come true!

Appendix

Appendix A: Kurti Buying Season Calendar

A detailed month-by-month guide highlighting the best times to stock up on specific styles, colours, and designs based on seasonal changes, festivals, and consumer buying patterns. This calendar helps retailers plan their inventory in advance, ensuring they always have the right mix of products to meet customer demand.

- ❖ **January-March:** Focus on spring collections; light fabrics and pastel colours.
- ❖ **April-June:** Stock up on summer essentials; vibrant colours and breathable materials.
- ❖ **July-September:** Prepare for monsoon and early autumn; waterproof and transitional pieces.
- ❖ **October-December:** Festive and winter collections; richer fabrics and deeper colours.

Appendix B: Key Indian Festivals and Kurti Sales

This overview of major Indian festivals outlines the types of kurtis that are popular during these celebrations. Retailers can use this guide to plan their inventory around these events, ensuring their collections meet the festive demand and appeal to the celebratory spirit of their customers.

Diwali (Festival of Lights)

Opt for kurtis in bright, festive colours adorned with gold and silver embellishments, sequins, and traditional prints. Luxurious fabrics like silk and satin are preferred, reflecting the prosperity and joy of the festival.

- **Holi (Festival of Colors):** Focus on light, airy, and comfortable kurtis in white and other light shades that can handle the vibrant colours of Holi. Fabrics that are easy to wash and care for, like cotton and linen, are ideal choices.

- **Navratri (Nine Nights):** This festival calls for colourful kurtis with extensive traditional embroidery, mirror work, and beadwork. Flared and layered kurtis in bright colours that symbolise the energy and vibrancy of Navratri are perfect.

- **Eid-ul-Fitr and Eid-ul-Adha:** Elegant kurtis in luxurious fabrics like velvet, chiffon, and georgette, featuring detailed embroidery and fine prints, cater to the festive mood. Soft pastels to rich jewel tones, adorned with intricate lace and beadwork, are suitable.

- **Raksha Bandhan (Bond of Protection):** Kurtis in soft, pastel shades with minimalistic designs and comfortable fabrics like cotton and georgette are ideal, reflecting the warmth and love between siblings.

- **Ganesh Chaturthi:** For this auspicious occasion, choose kurtis in vibrant hues with traditional motifs like elephants. Fabrics that offer comfort during the long hours of festivities, such as cotton and silk, are preferred.

- **Durga Puja:** Opt for kurtis in rich reds and oranges, symbolising the power and grace of Goddess Durga. Silks and handloom fabrics with traditional Bengali embroidery or prints are highly sought after.

- **Karva Chauth:** Saree-style or Anarkali kurtis in reds, maroons, and pinks, adorned with sequins, zari, and lace work, reflect the romantic essence of the festival.

- **Pongal/Sankranti (Harvest Festival):** Earthy tones and cotton kurtis with traditional South Indian weaves or prints, such as checks and stripes, celebrate the agrarian spirit of the festival.

Each of these festivals has its unique themes and aesthetic preferences, influencing fashion trends and consumer choices. Retailers should consider these preferences when curating their festive collections to ensure they resonate with the cultural and celebratory aspects of each occasion. Also, keep in mind the vacations season; Indian consumers spend a lot during vacations on casual dresses. Matching your store's offerings with the festive calendar not only makes shopping more enjoyable but also increases sales because you're providing exactly what people are looking for during these busy shopping times.

Appendix C: Supplier Contact List

A curated list of trusted suppliers who specialise in various types of kurtis, from traditional to modern fusion wear. This list includes contact information, specialty areas, and tips on value delivery and building lasting partnerships with these suppliers.

- ❖ **Traditional Wear Suppliers:** Contacts for suppliers specialising in classic kurti designs and regional specialties.

- ❖ **Modern and Fusion Wear Suppliers:** Information on suppliers who offer contemporary and fusion kurti designs.

Supplier Name	Contact	City	Specialisation Area

Notes:

Notes: